The Killer of Success: 3 Powerful Weapons to Overcome Excuses, Laziness and Procrastination

Frank K. Dixon

All rights reserved. No part of this publication may be reproduced, distributed, or transmitted in any form or by any means, including photocopying, recording, or other electronic or mechanical methods, without the prior written permission of the publisher, except in the case of brief quotations embodied in critical reviews and certain other noncommercial uses permitted by copyright law.

Copyright © Frank K. Dixon, 2022

Table of Contents

Chapter One

Excuses

Six excuses you must avoid

- ❖ I don't know how
- ❖ I'm afraid
- ❖ I don't have enough time
- ❖ I don't have enough money
- ❖ It's too late for me
- ❖ It's too hard

Chapter Two

Laziness

Three steps to start early and become successful

- ❖ Know where you want to be, not where you are

- Understand the metrics required to get there
- Pursue the success metrics that matter in the long run and go easy on the insignificant ones

Chapter Three

Procrastination

Eight Dreadful Effects of Procrastination
- Losing precious time
- Blowing opportunities
- Not Meeting Goals
- Ruining a career
- Lower self esteem
- Making poor decisions
- Negative
- Risking your health

INTRODUCTION

Stop making excuses, confront your anxieties, and have faith in yourself. You are capable of doing exploits.

Laziness, excuses, and postponement. These three things are the main obstacles to success.

We all offer excuses. You know how simple it is to manufacture them? But each and every justification sets you back in your quest to improve yourself. You'll advance a lot faster once you grasp this and stop using every single one of your excuses.

Accept NO excuses and try to DO instead of DON'T!

Despite having the capacity to act or exert oneself, laziness is the inability or unwillingness to do so. Lack of discipline resulting from low self-confidence, a lack of self-esteem, a lack of positive recognition from others, a lack of enthusiasm in the activity or confidence in its efficacy are all possible causes of laziness.

Procrastination or vacillation are two ways that laziness might appear.

The greatest obstacle preventing you from waking up, making the proper choices, and leading the life you've imagined is procrastination. No more justifications, indolence, or procrastination today, tomorrow, or any other day after that. YOU CAN ACHIEVE THIS!

Arguments kill progress.

We all have goals and aspirations for the future. Many of us seem to get stuck and are unable to understand why the flowers of riches we planted have yet to bloom.

Our goal-chasing false-starts are frequently due to limiting beliefs, lies we tell ourselves, and justifications we give to others. Here are seven of the most common justifications we make to avoid achieving our objectives and, ultimately, failing. Continue reading if you're prepared for some sobering truths.

Chapter One

EXCUSES

Let's get the most common defense out of the way now in the hopes that it won't come up again. "I do not have the time" is a common expression that means, "This is not that essential to me right now." The truth is that everyone of us has the time to devote to the things that really important.

We have the time to play around on our smart phones and tablets and watch mindless television. I don't need to look at your schedule to know that you have the time because you are reading this blog article after probably spending an eternity exploring Facebook, Instagram, YouTube, or other websites.

Please understand that I am happy that you are reading this and would appreciate it if you continued to the finish. However, I need you to realize that the time you spend online might easily be used to take the baby steps necessary to get you closer to the big step you need to take. Therefore, if you read this and use the justification "I don't have time," please be more responsible.

We are given the same amount of time each day as Oprah Winfrey, Bill Gates, and Beyonce. We all share the magical number of twenty-four. If any of the aforementioned people had used this defense to further their objectives, we might not be able to identify them now. The only things we should claim we don't have time for are pessimistic individuals and pointless justifications.

On the path to achievement, self-doubt and anxiety frequently seep in. This is a typical reaction to pushing outside of your comfort zone and shouldn't be a reason to stop; rather, it should serve as reassurance that you are on the correct track. Go back to the drawing board and raise the bar if you've set goals that don't make you feel threatened. You owe it to yourself.

Fear and self-doubt are hideous beasts, and your achievement is their favorite feast. If you want to achieve, you can't let these emotions hold you back. You are not only capable of doing what you have set out to do, but no one else can do it better than you. Please trust that whatever is on your heart is intended only for you and no one else. Your path to success will be paved if you face your fear and move forward anyway.

We must stop feeding ourselves the lie that we are unworthy of happiness and start telling ourselves, "I deserve it all."

We have all heard the old adage, "Don't put off tomorrow, what can be done today." Why push our goals further and further away when we can get to them now? Not soon. Not tomorrow. Now.

If something is important to you, and living the life of your dreams should be, then roll up your sleeves and get to work immediately. No excuses allowed in the Goal Chasers' Club.

Here's the thing, having zilch in your wallet sucks. I get it, but we have two choices here, to complain about it or to wake up and do something about it.

The universe has an amazing way of partnering with us when we are on the road to chasing our dreams. Speaking ill about money problems never improves our finances and drains the energy of everyone around us who is forced to listen. We must make a way, not an excuse, if we wish to succeed. Get a new job. Ask for an increase. Cut Spending. Get on your knees and pray. Begin speaking abundance into your life. Whatever you do, do not complain or make excuses.

Steve Harvey, Daniel Craig (James Bond), Steve Jobs, Dr. Phil, Halle Berry and Tyler Perry have all been homeless. Despite what seemed to be the obvious (lack of money), they remained prisoners of hope and focused not on the lack, but on their potential to achieve. Now if that doesn't inspire you to quit complaining and chase your goals, I I'm not sure what will. "Life would pay whatever price you ask of it," Tony Robbins reportedly remarked. Do you have the right inquiries?

We must decide for ourselves whether the benefit of realizing our wildest goals justifies the price of a little hard work. Nobody ever promised a smooth journey, and what fun is a road without a few detours?

The bumps, stumbles, and falls must be seen for what they are: opportunities for growth (if we learn from them) and fascinating tales to tell once we have overcome them. The most feeble excuse is to say that something is "too hard." Consider all of the challenging situations that you never imagined you would encounter.

It all comes down to how badly we desire something. No amount of effort (and most definitely no flimsy justifications) will prevent us from accomplishing our goals if we have a strong desire to do so.

People who adopt the "What's meant for me, will be for me" philosophy of life and don't take the required steps to achieve their goals are deluding themselves. Really hoping this isn't you. Although I firmly think that I should accept and receive all intended for me, I am even more of an advocate for actively assisting what is intended for me.

You would immediately get up out of your seat if a million bucks were across town for you.

Wouldn't you instantly get off your bum and take whatever steps are necessary to get there? Even if your aim is to lose 100 pounds rather than money, the basic idea is still the same. Take the steps required to arrive there. One of the first stages to realizing any desire is goal setting.

Be smart; set goals and take action. If you do this, success will come to you quickly.

You will undoubtedly run into plenty of doubters and Negative Nancies on your path to success who will be evaluating your every action, but you cannot let this deter you.

People that are successful encourage one another and recognize that success is a team effort. People who don't actively pursue their goals in life

Six excuses you must kill

You've made the decision that 2021 will be the year of your life's acceleration! You're certain that things will be different this time. You won't give up. You won't become disengaged. You'll follow through on your resolution to make a fresh start. You could have even made it your New Year's resolve. Sadly, you're not likely to succeed. The truth is that very few people actually follow through on their resolutions. According to University of Scranton studies, only 8% of people succeed in achieving their New Year's resolutions. What unifies these things? EXCUSES.

Most people find it much simpler to consider how something cannot be done than how it can be done. Many of us have a number of justifications on hand that we can use in an emergency. The main reasons we give for our actions are to defend ourselves and to explain our current situation. But these preconceived notions restrict our prospects of achievement. Consider the following justifications and commit to the fixes:

1. "I DON'T KNOW HOW." This popular justification gives you license to quit up completely.

• ACTION: Seek assistance. Never before in human history have there been as many resources and as much information available. You want to launch a charity. Thousands of books have been written about it. You must shed 100 pounds.

Thousands of CDs, movies, and blogs are available to support you. Looking to switch careers? Speak with a mentor or coach. Alternately, just give it a shot and see what happens.

2. "I'M AFRAID," Who hasn't been hesitant to experiment, think outside the box, or step outside their comfort zone? The majority of our

anxieties are social in nature and have no practical implications.

- ANSWER: Consider the worst scenario that could occur. Once you've identified the worst-case situations, you'll see that the dread is merely a ruse designed to crush your aspirations and stunt your development. Then, make a list of the best scenarios. You'll come to see that the anxieties preventing you from succeeding are more significant.

3. "I DON'T HAVE ENOUGH TIME." If your heart is in it then you will make the time for what's truly important to you.

- **SOLUTION:** Create a list of the things you do on a daily basis from the moment you wake up until the end of the day. Record your activities in fifteen-minute blocks. Include everything from talking on the phone, to surfing the Internet, to watching television. After doing this for one week, most people are able to find at least three hours to dedicate to a new activity or adventure.

4. "I DON'T HAVE ENOUGH MONEY." There is usually a way to work around a lack of financial resources.

- **SOLUTION:** Find alternatives. For example, if you're looking to increase your skills but can't afford college tuition, there are other ways to enhance your credentials. For instance, volunteer at a non-profit organization, get certification in a particular skill, or intern for a small company on your days off. If you are business owner, consider bartering (trading your services or products). There is always a way. You just may have to work a little harder to find solutions to support your growth.

5. "IT'S TOO LATE FOR ME." It's never too late to become what you might have been. A person climbed Mount Everest in his eighties. People have gone back to medical school in their sixties. Getting a late start might be less convenient and more challenging, but there's nothing wrong with that.

- **SOLUTION:** Figure out what interests you, influences you, and motivates you. Build a plan for the challenges that are really important to you and take one step at a time to complete your goals.

6. "IT'S TOO HARD." Some endeavors are certainly more difficult than others. But claiming that something is "too hard" is really just another way of admitting that you're afraid. People with limited resources and talent can still be extremely successful.

- **SOLUTION:** Set your mind on success! Those with motivation and stamina are really the ones who succeed. Get an accountability partner. Read encouraging stories. Practice affirmations. Do what's necessary to keep your thoughts and energy centered on a successful outcome.

Chapter Two

LAZINESS

There's always going to be people smarter than you and people dumber than you.

Everyone wants to be successful in life. However, not everyone has what it takes to get there. Life is competitive, and to constantly keep up and excel over your peers is a tough and struggling battle.

Sure, some people believe that they can dominate everyone based on their natural abilities and intelligence, but you would be a fool to deny that there isn't someone smarter and stronger than you out there (if you happen to be that one person who truthfully qualifies for that, email me and I'll apologize to you personally).

For most of us, gambling that you are the ultimate genius is a risky way of winning any battle.

The only way to win is to spend more time more efficiently on it
For everyone who is not the ultimate genius, the only way to beat the genius is to spend more time more efficiently on that activity. You'll have to spend more time practicing, doing, failing, and learning than the born natural.

In his often-quoted book, Outliers, Malcom Gladwell talks about how in order to become highly successful in something, one needs to spend 10,000 hours on that specific task. To put this into perspective, this is like practicing a specific action four hours a day, seven days a week, for seven years. (speaking of which, how many hours did your last "social media expert" put into his expertise?)
Needless to say, spending more time on something is not enough, as HOW you spend your time on it matters a lot too. I used to play chess on Pogo.com a lot (until Snow Leopard doesn't support their java anymore...), and I've

seen people who have astonishingly played 14,000 games but still plays like a beginner. These people lack the fundamentals of chess and a good player can literally beat them without looking at the board .
Obviously, if you practice the wrong way, spending more hours doing something will only make you suck more. If you don't learn from your experiences every step of the way, you might as well not do it and die.

Now the problem with spending more hours against others is that everyone has a limited amount of time on a given day. Since most people have to spend time sleeping, eating (and some even have friends and family!), whatever you do can only be highly marginal.

If your average competitor spends 4 hours a day improving himself, it's pretty hard to three-times his effort and beat him that way. If you work your butt off, you probably practice 6 hours a day trying to get some kind of advantage. Yes, it works, and I encourage that if your goal is to become powerful in your field, but it's definitely an uphill battle.

In that case, the best way to outcompete is to wait for what I call the "Slacker's Gap." Basically, this is a time when your competitors are taking days off and relaxing. When they are active, it's incredibly hard to have a 40% advantage over them. But when they are doing nothing, you immediately gain immense ground since any progress you put in closes your difference by the same amount.

Am I telling you that in order to win, you need to be a workaholic and have less/no work-life balance?

I actually am. If you truly want to become powerful and influential in your field, you have to do more than what others are doing. Sure, there's this thing about working smarter, not harder, 4-hour-work-week and all that. But to become highly competitive, you need to work smart AND hard. You need to do the 4-hour-work-week, 80 hours a week.

If you want to accomplish uncommon things in your life, you need to live everyday of your life uncommonly. If you spend your day like everyone else, you will end up like everyone else. It's that simple. Starting early allows you to stay competitive and become successful the easy way

But there's actually an easy way to take advantage of the Slacker's Gap. Lets say instead of working 50% more than everyone else, you started a year before everyone. That means for an entire year, your competitors are zero, and whatever hours you put in will be more than infinite times what they are doing. This is not just a Slacker's Gap, this is a Slacker's Valley. No one is there to challenge you until they realize they should start too.

Once you've had a head start like that, when your competitors start, they need to work their butts off, while you simply need to maintain steady pace to keep your lead. Life is easy and non stressful that way, obviously until some workaholic competitor surpasses you while you are in your Slacker's Gap.

Three Steps to start early and become successful

Everything is easier said than done. HOW do you actually start earlier? If it was that easy than everyone would be doing it already! Here I lay out a few steps to help you gain an early bird advantage.

1. KNOW where you want to be, not where you are

Most people just focus on the present and their needs right now. You shouldn't do that. You want to think about exactly where you want to be years from now.

Have you ever met people who are "lucky" because they knew what they wanted to do at a very young age? Most of them did not become "lucky" because they sat on their butts. They probably actively tried out a lot of things, got exposed to a variety of interests, and finally found out what they are passionate about.

In the same way, you need to spend a lot of time trying different things and really envisioning yourself 5 years later. Instead of handling the tasks at hand, really spend time figuring out what does success mean to you 5 to 10 years later. Yes, it could be daunting, but if you want to become successful, this gives you an immense advantage that is too precious to not take advantage of.

This is actually the hardest part of taking advantage of the Slacker's Valley and requires a lot of initiative, speculation, outside advice and soul-searching. The rest is a lot more systematic.

2. Understand the metrics required to to get there

Once you know where you want to be many years from now, you have to figure out what are the metrics that matter verses the ones that don't.

For instance, if you are a dental student who just wants to be a General Dentist, passing dental school is very important, but getting top grades is not (it is if you want to specialize). Of course you want to make sure you nailed down all your dental skills in order to treat patients well, but you don't have to kill yourself over classes like Biochemistry or such.

However, what does matter for a successful dentist is how many people in your practicing city know about your service and thinks positively of you. A dentist's success is not measured by how well how he did in school or even how good he is at dentistry. It's measured by how many patients he can attract and retain to his practice. That's why established dentists have an advantage over younger dentists, even if some of them may not have done better in school nor are they necessarily better at what they do.

This immediately means that networking and building a personal brand to a future patient-base is much more important for a dental student than getting perfect scores in school. It's really important to identify what are the metrics that matter verses the ones that seem important at the moment.

3. Pursue the success metrics that matter in the longrun and go easy on the insignificant ones

Once you realize what metrics truly matter, you need to start preparing for that immediately, no matter how many years later would it start to matter.

Most dental students would only focus on studying and hanging out with other dental students when they're still in school. The FD student on the other hand would spend time networking with others and establishing herself as a future dentist to all sorts of demographics in her target city.

That way once she actually starts a practice, people already know about her practice and would contact her whenever they or their friends are looking for a new dentist. Even better, while in school she should probably network with those that don't have a personal dentist yet but would be looking for one a couple years later, like those still in other professional schools.

As you can see, in this example it is also very important for the dental student to know exactly which CITY she wants to practice, since for a dentist it only matters that people who are local know about what she does.

If the city the dental students wants to practice in is not the city she is studying at, what she needs to do is instantly network with people in that city via online methods. Use social networking sites and tools like Twitter or Yelp to establish relationships with people in that city while constantly letting them know she is an aspiring dentist might yield great benefits later on when you update them, "I'm finally a Dentist now and am opening a practice in Orange County!"

She can even start a blog that targets the local audience there like a food/restaurant rating blog (would need some research or a friend's help) to get locals to read her stuff on a regular basis, while having a "About me" section that talks about how she will become a dentist.
All in all, when you know what are the future metrics that matter, you need to immediately get

off your ass and start building that foundation while others are oblivious of this.

This "lazy" way to become successful is HARD!

Now at this point you might be contesting, "Didn't you say that this was the LAZY man's way of winning? This is SOO much work!" It's true. In order to become powerful in your field, you have to put in tons of work. There's no way out of it. But some people spend their entire lives working hard and never get to where they want to be. This post is more about using a realistic and doable way to get an advantage over others without killing yourself.

Based on how ambitious you truly are, by no means should you really just get an early start and chillax from there. Remember that the difference between 95 and 96 is not 1. If everyone else is a 95 and you are a 96, you are the winner, and the winner gets all the opportunities. In a winner takes all situation, it's the difference between 0 and 100. If you truly want to become the best at what you do, you need to start early and constantly make sure you are on top of your game.

What if I'm already behind?

You're screwed. Haha, not necessarily. Since most people are still slackers and don't take much action, you actually have a huge chance of catching up in most fields. All you have to do is after you read things like this blog or some other self-improvement book, actually convert it to action and DO SOMETHING. Most people read this kind of stuff just to feel good and agree with things, but only the 1% of the people who actually follow through and make it happen are the winners. The key to winning is not starting early, it's being proactive in empowering your own life however way you can whenever you can. There's a reason why "Be Proactive" is the first chapter of the 7 Habits of Highly Successful People.
Everyone else is still sitting in the sidelines. Be a winner and start now.

Chapter Three

PROCASTINATION

The negative effects of procrastination can range from simply missing a deadline on an important task to something more long-term, such as a missed opportunity that kills a dream. Some of us might be lucky enough to identify our tendency to procrastinate in time and still do something about it.

For others, it can have long-lasting effects that resonate throughout their lives.

Procrastination varies from person to person and is not always obvious. Sometimes, it is a hidden fear that we don't want to acknowledge, or it could even be as simple as not wanting to do something because it just doesn't motivate us.

Procrastinating behaviors appear at various levels, the extreme of which is chronic procrastination. Chronic procrastination can also result from mental health issues, eating disorders, ADHD, anxiety, and depression.[1]

Whatever the reason may be, if you know you are a procrastinator, you should be careful, as it has far more damaging effects than you may realize.

8 Dreadful Effects of Procrastination

1. Losing Precious Time
How much time have you wasted procrastinating?

The worst thing about procrastinating is the moment you realize that you are two, five, or ten years older, and nothing has changed.

This is a terrible feeling because you can't turn back the hands of time; you have to live with the helpless feeling of regret. There is nothing worse than feeling frustrated at yourself, knowing the situation could have been so different if only you had taken that first step.

2. Blowing Opportunities
Studies have shown that people lose about 26 days each year because of their procrastinating behaviors.[2]

How many opportunities have you wasted because you didn't take advantage of them when they were there? This is when the effects of procrastination make you really want to kick yourself.

What you don't realize is that the opportunity could have been life changing, but you missed out on it. Most opportunities only come around once; you are never guaranteed a second chance.

Opportunities are the world's way of giving you more, so do yourself a favor and grab them with both hands as soon as they present themselves.

3. Not Meeting Goals
Procrastination seems to come on with full force when we entertain the thought of goals, of wanting to achieve or change something. You might have a strong desire to change, but you just can't seem to take the first step forward.

This is normally confusing and perplexing; you might find yourself thinking, "Why is it so hard to go for something that I want so badly?" Only you can answer that; you'll have to explore a little deeper into the resistance.

We set goals because we have a deep desire to better our lives in some way. If you don't do this because of procrastination, you reduce the possibility to better your life.

Too Overwhelmed to Achieve What You Need to Do?
Get the push you need to move forward by grabbing your **FREE** action plan to end overwhelm, regain motivation and get your life together!

Uncover the root cause behind your procrastination if it's preventing you from achieving your goals, or you may never attain them.

4. Ruining a Career

The way you work directly affects your results, how much you achieve, and how well you perform, so the effects of procrastination can end up being detrimental to your career.

Procrastination may prevent you from meeting deadlines or achieving your monthly targets. What consequence will this eventually have on your career?

You might miss out on promotions or even be at risk of losing your job. You can try to hide it for a while, but don't doubt that long-term procrastination at work will almost certainly ruin your career.

5. Lower Self-Esteem

This is one of the vicious circles you might find yourself in. We tend to procrastinate because low self-esteem makes us feel that we won't be able to get a task or project done the right way. Unfortunately, procrastinating only increases feelings of low self-esteem, making us doubt ourselves even more.

One study involving 426 college students found that "academic procrastination was negatively predicted by self-esteem, and self-control."[3]

When we have low self-esteem, we hold ourselves back, feel unworthy of success, and begin self-sabotaging. Procrastination eats away your confidence, slowly but surely.

If this resonates with you, focus on building your self-esteem instead of holding on to the illusion that you should be able to do something, as this makes you force yourself into something when you are not ready.

6. Making Poor Decisions
Poor decision making is one of the worst effects of procrastination. When you procrastinate, you make decisions based on criteria that most likely wouldn't be there if you didn't procrastinate, like pressure to *finally* make a decision because time is running out.

Emotions heavily influence the decisions we make, and procrastination increases negative emotions, which can push us into making decisions that don't serve us in the long run.

Instead of rushing through decisions while procrastinating, write out all the possibilities and find a calm moment to analyze the pros and cons of each.

7. Negative Impact on Your Reputation

Nobody wants empty promises, therefore it hurts your reputation when you continually stating you'll do something but don't. You harm not only your reputation but also your confidence and self-worth. You'll notice that each time you put something off, it gets simpler because you are no longer shocking yourself.

People may cease relying on you and refrain from giving you opportunities if they are concerned that you would put things off and leave them to clean up the mess. You can change your reputation as a procrastinator, even if you already have one. The next time someone asks you to accomplish something, make use of all of your resources to finish it promptly. Your reputation will start to increase each time you complete a task, which will open up new opportunities and improve your connections with those around you.

8. Risking Your Health
Among the effects of procrastination are mental health problems like stress and anxiety, and these in turn are linked to health issues. If your procrastination leads to feelings of depression, this will start to affect other areas of your life.

If you procrastinate too much with something, it will most likely start to stress you out and cause anxiety, especially when other people or things are involved, and all of this can lead to poor health outcomes.

Another way that procrastination can affect your health in the short term is when you continually put off check-ups and postpone appointments or things you need to do, such as exercise. The problem only gets worse and the consequences direr.

Final Reflections

Although the consequences of procrastination may not first appear to be all that severe, they can eventually lead to tension, worry, dashed hopes, and low self-esteem. Develop time management skills so you can deal with procrastination as it arises rather than letting it rule your life.

Researchers found that cognitive behavioral therapy considerably reduced procrastination and "reduced procrastination more strongly than the other types of interventions" in a study on procrastination remedies.

CONCLUSION

Your success depends on how hard you work. No activity yields no outcomes. As you work toward your objective, divide your tasks into manageable tasks. Changes need to be made now. Although transformation isn't always simple, it's essential to your success. Remind yourself of the motivations behind your initial efforts. And have the guts to abandon your justifications and pursue what you genuinely desire. You'll be happy that you did!

There is no mistake in success. A careful emphasis on continually taking the steps necessary to accomplish your objectives, no matter how big or small, will lead to incredible achievement. There are only a select few who rise to the challenge to pursue their dreams with passion and perseverance; there are no unintentionally successful people in the world. Only a select few people rise to the challenge of relentlessly pursuing their dreams. But make no mistake, there is a recipe for success; passion and commitment alone are not sufficient. The formula is effective; it has always been effective and will remain effective for as long as the world exists.

Therefore, the most intelligent among us are aware of one fact that is extremely clear: this. Modeling the style of thinking of someone who has successfully traveled the path you're trying to walk is the quickest method to get from where you are to where you want to be. By imitating the behaviors of the world's most successful individuals, you may put your life and business on a fast road to extraordinary success. The blueprint provides you with useful information and straightforward actions you can follow right away to immediately improve your life and unquestionably advance your business.

www.ingramcon.ent.com/pod-product-compliance
Lightning Source LLC
Chambersburg PA
CBHW050321220526
45465CB00005B/2077